Paddy Cunneen [illegible] worked extensively as a c[illegible], Ireland and on Broadwa[illegible] runs to some two hundred productions for the NT, RSC, Cheek By Jowl, Donmar Warehouse, Abbey and Druid Theatres, Liverpool Everyman, and many others. In addition he composes for BBC Radio Drama, RTE Radio Drama and has a number of TV and film credits. He was Bafta nominated for his score to the Channel 4 film *Boy A*. He has written two plays for BBC radio, *Sunburst Finish* (with Andrea Gibb) and *Disenchantment*, and one other stage play, *The Waltz Of The Cold Wind*.

Marjorie
0785 182 8844

if lost, please ring.

fairplay press

Fleeto

by Paddy Cunneen

fairplay press

First published by fairplay press, an imprint of Capercaillie Books Limited in 2009.

Registered office 1 Rutland Court, Edinburgh.

Printed in the UK.

A catalogue record for this book is available from the British Library.

ISBN 978-1-906220-28-0

Introduction

Political Theatre from Greece to Glasgow

In Ancient Greece the theatre served a central role in the religious and political life of the state. Performances formed part of the annual festivities in honour of the mysterious god of revels, Dionysus. An altar dedicated to the god stood centre stage and was integrated into the action; and the whole adult community attended each play, from law-givers, policy makers and merchants to craftspeople, manual labourers, soldiers and slaves. The dominant dramatic genre, the tragedy, took its story-lines from the history of Greece as commemorated in the epics of Homer and his imitators. Its plots were imprinted in the blood of the spectators, so that everyone knew the outcome of each incident and groaned with sympathetic pain as the familiar narrative (one might call it the family narrative) unspooled itself afresh before their horrified eyes. By the end, not only had the audience relived a portion of the past; they had also been reminded of how that past inhabited their lives here and now, of how the repercussions of the events they had seen were still being worked out in contemporary Athens: in the relationships between themselves and their gods, in the continuing cycles of conflict between generations and states, in the laws that sought to prevent a repetition of the terrible crimes and errors of their ancestors.

How can we possibly emulate such an intensely political theatre in the twenty-first century? Quite simply, it can't be done. Bloodshed was banned from the Athenian stage because the theatre was a holy site and the altar of the god must not be contaminated. Now, by contrast, we hardly feel we have witnessed a scene of fear and horror unless blood gets copiously spilled on it. For the Greeks, tragedy was what led up to the outbreak of violence, the dilemmas that led people rationally and emotionally to condone it. Tragedy was also what followed on from the orgy of destruction; the divine and human retribution, in economic terms the cost of that orgy, which manifests itself above all in the torment of guilt and grief that afflicts its participants, and which continues to be paid with interest by their descendants as murder spawns retaliatory murder from one lifetime to the next. For the citizens of the twenty-first century, on the other hand, tragedy is the violent event itself: the plane crash, the knife thrust, the shooting of an innocent bystander. We're not very good with causes or consequences, not very capable of sustaining our sympathy with victims – and certainly not with perpetrators – for more than the few brief minutes when the news item arrests our attention. Images are important to us, and if there aren't eye-catching pictures of a tragic occurrence we are barely capable of imagining it, of internalizing it, of pondering how it relates to our often comfortable lives. We can, however, learn from the Greeks, if we want to.

By turning away from the violent incident, by focusing on what happens at the periphery – before and after an atrocity, not at the moment of its unfolding – the Greeks discovered how to measure its impact on the community. Central to this process of discovery is the Chorus. A group of twelve or more onlookers – usually ordinary people, old men or young women with little or no say in the running of the state – serve as commentators on the tragic situation: commentators who are intensely engaged with the story while never taking a hand in it, or even witnessing its events at first hand. They ask the protagonists questions, urge them to act or refrain from acting, puzzle with them over the impossible choices that face them, weep with them after the choices have been made. And they mediate between protagonist and audience, guiding our reactions by example – teaching us, in fact, how to be co-narrators, how to help make a performance happen, as all theatre audiences do through their audible, visible reactions to events on stage . . .

The Chorus represents the ripples that spread outwards from any given outbreak of aggression. The Chorus speaks or sings in verse, like all speakers in Greek tragedy; but their verse is more formally organized, more repetitive, more ritualistic than the dialogue of the protagonists. As a result, they initiate the process of coping with atrocity, of meditating on it, of finding a way finally to escape its repercussions, perhaps even to stop it happening again. The Chorus reminds us that no atrocity happens to an isolated individual, and thus offers hope that each atrocity may in the end, against all likelihood, strengthen rather than undermine the community that suffers it, as verse strengthens a narrative by giving it rhythm and shape.

What else can we learn from Greek tragedy? A good deal about the relationship between the sexes, about how the politics of the state is intimately related with the politics of gender and the home. This lesson is learned through the centrality of women to the tragic tradition – a centrality that's astonishingly at odds with the physical absence of women from the Athenian stage.

One of the strangest things to modern eyes about the theatre of ancient Greece – as with the theatre of Shakespeare's England – is that no women were permitted to perform in it, no doubt as a result of certain taboos set in place by a long-established patriarchy. Yet women figure prominently in these community plays – perhaps because they kept communities together while men were away making war. They perform shocking actions: Clytemnestra murders her husband in his bath, Electra kills her mother, Medea her children, as if to assert their dominance of the familial environment these actions violate. But women are also those, like Electra or Antigone, who are left behind when the action is over, or is happening elsewhere. They are Cassandra, the prisoner of war whose gift of prophecy gives her dreadful access to all the atrocities of the future as well as of the past; Iphigenia, who must be sacrificed at the gods' behest before the action of the Trojan war can begin; or Clytemnestra, whose resentment builds up over the ten long years when her soldier husband is away fighting Trojans and getting written about by epic poets. Women live the consequences of violence in the household, while men hurry off into exile to experience those consequences as private suffering, an egotistic path to glory as destructive as making war. It's women, then, who stand in the vanguard of resistance to the self-centred power politics – ostensibly based on the highest principles – which men have made their own. This is why, in the 1940s, Jean Anouilh and Bertolt Brecht chose the tragedy of Antigone, the woman who stood alone against the tyranny of Cleon, as a means of articulating resistance to Nazism in occupied France and wartime Germany. Her situation seemed to them to be utterly pertinent to their period, ravaged as it was by global conflict. And in *Fleeto*, Paddy Cunneen finds Greek tragedy still to be utterly pertinent to the urban warfare of the twenty-first century.

Like Aeschylus' Agamemnon, *Fleeto* centres on the dire consequences of the association between masculinity and violence. Thirst for revenge sets the violence in motion, as young men roam the city streets looking for payback after the disfigurement of one of their friends. Their exhilaration at the prospect of violence is conveyed through the driving rhythms of blank verse, the medium of epic poetry in English as most famously deployed by Milton. Their rampage through the town is monitored by a world-weary Chorus: a policeman or member of the 'polis' as they say in Glasgow (polis in Greek means city-state), whose origins as a young man trained up in violence (he's an ex-soldier) enables him both to understand their mounting excitement and to predict its terrible outcome. This polis-man, then, doubles the role of Prophet with that of Chorus; he's Cassandra or Tiresias as well as the Old Men of Argos. After the epic section of *Fleeto* – after violence has run its course – comes the transition to tragedy, as the young 'hero', avenger and perpetrator, finds himself faced with the consequences of his actions. Tormented by guilt yet still defiant, self-accusing yet also enraged by the culture that has shaped him, it's at this point that Cunneen's protagonist comes closest to the complexity of the protagonists of Aeschylus and Sophocles, trapped in a dilemma that finally – as the Chorus reminds us – is our own, not someone else's.

Greek tragedy found inspiration in the epics of Homer, and Cunneen draws on the last book of the *Iliad*, where King Priam travels to his enemies' camp to beg the dead body of his son from Achilles, who killed him in revenge for the death of a friend. Confronted by Priam, young Achilles finds that he shares with the old man a clear-eyed awareness of how they are caught up in a cycle of violence – the Trojan War – from which there's no escape. The pair shed tears for the loved ones they've lost, and all hostilities between the opposing armies are suspended for a moment, as if to enable the world of gods and men to participate in the horror and grief of this pair from different generations, to mourn with them a while before the cycle continues on its course. But *Fleeto's* equivalent of Priam is a woman, the mother of an innocent victim. Her status as the enemy of the man she confronts – her son's killer – is a function of class warfare, a more deep-rooted and insidious propagator of violence than any military campaign. And the questions she raises when she meets the young murderer, and the questions he asks of her, are as closely entwined with the lives of a twenty-first century audience as the events of Greek tragedy were entwined with the Athenian community that witnessed their first performances.

Fleeto was first written as part of a series of lunchtime plays at the Òran Mór in the West End of Glasgow. The series, billed as 'A Play, a Pie and a Pint', has become a regular feature of the weekly calendar for a section of the city, to the extent that Glasgow audiences have made it perhaps the biggest commissioner of new drama in Europe. Of course, the Oran Mor can hardly claim to be an all-embracing social institution like the theatre of Dionysus in Athens; but as a launching-pad for urban, political, inclusive theatre, there are few better venues in this epoch of ours. Let's hope the series continues to flourish and spawn imitators, on its own modest scale, with something of the vigour of tragedy in ancient Greece.

R. W. Maslen, Senior Lecturer,
University of Glasgow, 2009.

Characters

MACKIE:	A young lad from a housing scheme.
POLICE OFFICER	
KENZIE:	Leader of a gang of young men.
THE MOTHER:	A well to do woman whose teenage son James is murdered.
GANG:	Made up of Biscuit, Stu, Dunky, Whacker, Coyle and Div.

List of Scenes

Scene 1:	Slash And Invocation
Scene 2:	Sergeant Cunt
Scene 3:	The Ned Iliad
Scene 4:	Flight From The Scene
Scene 5:	Forensics
Scene 6:	Where Now?
Scene 7:	The Knock On The Door
Scene 8:	The Book
Scene 9:	Whose Tragedy?
Scene 10:	No Reasons
Scene 11:	Dog Borstal
Scene 12:	Petrol Station
Scene 13:	The Burger Bar
Scene 14:	Funeral Pyre

Scene 1

Slash and Invocation

MACKIE: No, not Wee Andy, No. Ya bastards. No.

POLICE OFFICER: With heavy heart I stand here once again.
To tell you yet another Glasgow lad
Was slashed and stabbed last night upon our streets.

MACKIE: Ah, Jesus fucking shit, this can't be true.

POLICE OFFICER: Young Andrew Graham . . .

MACKIE: Wee Andy, he's been killed!

POLICE OFFICER: . . . While walking home alone just after school.
Was by a gang of mindless youths with knives,
Most viciously attacked and left for dead.

MACKIE: Wee Andy never done naebody harm,
He never got in trouble or a fight.

POLICE OFFICER: At first we feared that he would lose his life;
so grievous were the injuries sustained . . .

MACKIE: He hardly ever went outside his house
We two just hung out at his place all day
And played Olympus War Gods on PC.
And noo my pal's been stabbed. Fur whi'?

POLICE OFFICER: But Glasgow has such skill in stab wound care –
For all too much we practise now this craft –
That surgeon's blade and stitch has saved that life
Which thuggish blade last night put under threat.
I want to introduce his mother now, who will
Appeal for public help in tracking down
The perpetrators of this sickening deed.

MACKIE: His maw is greeting sore, she cries and howls.

The recorded voice of Andy's Mother is played.

See now they've slashed and scarred ma poor boy's face?
All swollen like a ham hock tied wi' string,
He's marked for life. He might as well be dead.
Who's gonnae give him work, or teach him skills
'Cept dealers, druggies, thieves and life's sick dregs?

MACKIE: She's right! She's fuckin' right. Who cares 'bout him?

POLICE OFFICER: We have some footage from CCTV
Which shows a group of four young men that hour
Close to the scene of crime – all walking past.
And here we must say categorically,
That they are clearly not involved in this.
Now, most of them are Asian, it would seem,
We simply need to speak . . .

MACKIE: Power of man and manhood, roar and yell
Across grey tenements, as on that day
When Kenzie and his troops broke running free,
Poured petrol on the cinders of their shame,
And blazed their way, unstoppable and strong,
In brotherhood and clans of valiant troops
Imposing on the place their Ways of War –
And made the toon respect them by dread deeds
Of wrath and blood let loose upon its streets;
Bellow in me now and fill my veins
Wi' rage and lust for vengeance, since the state,
Wi' haughty hand and Asbo law enforced,
Would sty me in these schemes of filth and grime
Wherein I will, enslaved, fast waste away
Unless, wi' fearless chib, I stake their hearts
And teach those cunts who slashed Wee Andy's face,
Tae fear my kind and count me as a man.

Scene 2

Sergeant Cunt

POLICE OFFICER: I feared the worst would happen in this case.
See, we have here so many gangs of youths
Which gather in large groups and carry knives
And seek revenge according to their Code –
A cruel code, requiring blood for blood.
I made appeal for calm on TV news.

KENZIE: So, on ma fucking screen, some Sergeant Cunt
Calls out to me and asks me to stay calm.

POLICE OFFICER: I ask for calm maturity today
Especially from those young men in our town
Who take the law, and knife, in their own hands
And rampage through the streets in violent gangs.
Come out and meet the world, full man-to-man
Not cowering in ranks of hooded thugs.
It's only what a man can face alone
That is the truest measure of his worth.

KENZIE: **(to POLICE OFFICER)**
'Ya fuckin prick, ya! Bawbag of the law!'
(To audience.)
Who hides, beneath a chibproof vest of black,
A heart still blacker yet – it throbs
In frustrate rage tae pan my fucking face.
He rants at me now, 'Braveheart, stand alone!'
Whilst on his collar sits a radio
Wi' access tae full powers of the State
And reinforcements swiftly motioned in.
(To POLICE OFFICER.)
'Then stand alone yersel, ya cuntin' fuck!'

POLICE OFFICER: I'm sick at heart for what will happen next,
There's little that can stop young men like him.
He's smart, he's sharp. He'll organise a gang
Of running youths for violent revenge.

KENZIE: **(running off)** Ya wanker!

POLICE OFFICER: Enraged by injured pride and out for blood,
They'll go berserk with knives on city streets
Till someone pays a forfeit – with their life.

Scene 3

The Ned Iliad

MACKIE: Next. Kenzie came and found me by the shop,
He walked right up wi' can of brew in hand
And eyeballed me tae let me know the score.

KENZIE: So you're wee Andy's pal. Here. Come wi' me.

MACKIE: He threw away the fag from aff his lips
And beckoned me tae follow wi' his hand.
So round behind the wall we went as one.

KENZIE: We're gonnae sort those cunts who hurt your pal –
Cos they deserve whatever comes their way
For cutting up Wee Andy's face wi' knives.
Naebody gets away wi' shit like that,
See, naebody touches naebody from our scheme.
We take care of our own, we get them back.
Come and join wi' us and get them cunts.
I'll teach ya how tae break their fuckin heids.
If it's Asylum that those fuckers seek,
We'll put them in a madhouse right enough.

MACKIE: And then he reached inside his trackie top
And pulled, wi' skillful hand in deadly grip,
That Blade – most mortal of all blades on Earth –
It sliced the air apart, like shrieking ice,
The way a plane will scrat the bastard sky.

KENZIE: This blade we grabbed from poxy Eastend hands,
When proudly came a gang of Fuckin' Neds
From Dennistoun tae mix it on our patch;
They took sore blows that day, some fuckin wounds.
Not one big man of theirs escaped our wrath
But left Infirmary sheets stained black wi' blood.
It greeted from the slashes in their flesh –
As if their meat be-wept their sorry luck
Tae war 'gainst such BraveHeart lads as we.
And homewards were they sent tae think again.

MACKIE: Is this the blade that sliced up that guy's hand?

KENZIE: Aye, fuckin' Jezza came from South Nitshill
Tae spray his bastard menchie on our walls.
That cunt he tried his best tae save his face
Against my slashing rage last August night.
Two fingers from his haun he lost right there
When savage blade in righteous anger ripped
That haun apart, and severed bone from bone.
Two dying digits left upon the street.
Which Div and Stu picked up in scornful glee
And gave, in mocking fists, the finger back
Tae that cunt greetin' on the ground in pain.

MACKIE: Then Kenzie, holding high this vengeful blade,
Began tae call the brothers tae his side.

KENZIE: Come on!

A gang of six young men suddenly run on stage shouting.

MACKIE: And wi' his other haun aloft he crossed
A carving knife, as lethal as the first,
So made a metal saltire of the pair.
This filled the troops wi' joy . . .

The GANG shout out loud in malevolent joy.

. . . and then he spoke
In these proud words of war – for all tae hear.

KENZIE: We're gonnae stick these blades into those cunts,
Deep in their chests, right through their fuckin hearts . . .

GANG: Yeah!

KENZIE: We're gonnae let their scummy lifeblood drain
Into the mingin' Clyde, whose filthy flow
Will retch and vomit up in rank distaste
At foreign life-juice, polluting foul
The manky turds and condoms in her flood . . .

GANG: Great! Wa-hey!

MACKIE: And so he spoke – or words tae that effect,
At which, like monkey hordes in war-lust thrill,
The chatter and the patter sounded out
From all the troops now ready for the fray . . .

GANG: Yeah! Fuckin' right!

MACKIE: So Stu proclaimed aloud of how he would,
'Wi' Timbie boot, stamp on some wanker's face
And spread his nose in bright red bloody smear
Across his mooth, when emptied of its teeth.'

The GANG gives a short burst of wild laughter. One gang member jumps up on stage and mimes as MACKIE describes Biscuit's actions.

MACKIE: Then up rose Biscuit, he that can out-run
The fastest footed polis, or his dug,
And round the troops his dance of war began –
Wi' arms a whirl of menace round his heid . . .

GANG: **(all shout)** Ya fanny!

MACKIE: And though some shouted 'fanny' as he danced,
Yet all were full of joy within their hearts . . .
Then Dunky, Stevo, Whacker, Coyle and Div, . . .

The GANG points at one of their number and calls out to him.

GANG: Divv-oh!

MACKIE: Whose fame extends frae Greenock tae Lyndale
For 'Causin It at every fuckin chance',
Began tae chant,

Under MACKIE's speech, The GANG quietly begin to sing following to the tune of *Auld Lang Syne*.

GANG: Go hame, ya cunts, Go hame, ya cunts.
Away tae fuck, Go hame!

MACKIE: . . . which stirred
the Fleeto Hearts
Til all were pure dead mento for the deed –
Tae slay the needy, piss-bag foreign scum.
The locusts in our homeland – on our broo.

This song they sang, and all the troops joined in –

The GANG suddenly bursts in to a deafening chorus.

GANG: Go hame ya cunts, go hame ya cunts,
Away tae fuck, go hame!

MACKIE: Then, straight away, wi' combat mind and will –
As being brothers all in Burbry's clan –
Bright helmets of pale Tartan we put on,
Their peaks turned skyward in a jaunty slant
That gives the finger tae the Gods above;
And some their cowls and hoods of war raised up,
Tae veil their visage from the Cyclops Eye –
That keeps its snidey watch, by video,
From pillars and tall masts about the toon.

The GANG make mocking cries as they make obscene gestures at the camera.

MACKIE: And checked we then our weapons for the job –
Our breadknives, chisels, hammers, stanleys, clubs,
Our apple corers – fit tae punch a hole . . .

GANG: Owwwffff!

MACKIE: From which some fucker's blood would drain in floods
Of liquid death on tarmac under him.
Some said hot machetes they could get
Whose weight, when swung in battle's fiercest rage,
Will sever flesh and veins and shatter bone,
But some said they would never carry knives –
Tae risk four years of life in Polmont Jail?
When they, wi' boot or fist, could haud their own
And crack some mad cunt's skull or gouge his eye.

So chibs and claymores – all were then concealed
In Jaket, trackies, socks, or Chantelle's purse –
Like sgian dubh in ancient times – obscured
In deadly hiding place from rival's eye.

GANG: Come Ahead! Ya Bas!

MACKIE: And next we searched, on darkened Glasgow streets,
Tae find a leech on Caledonia's heart.

A Black Watch we would keep until we found
Some foreign cunt, who'd left his own backyard,
Tae live the bluebell life wi' Scotland's best?

GANG: Aye Right! No Way! Etc

MACKIE: Through Merchant Streets we prowled and bayed like
wolves,
That, wi' the scent of blood, will leave behind
Their natural habitation tae commit
Their darkest deeds in city's darkest lanes.

And driven wi' this hunger, we raced on
Tae hunt and harry down, in rightful wrath,
Stray members of that evil Asian breed.
Then, finding one such cunt alone, we swarmed
Tae pann his stupit melt right there and then . . .

GANG: Ya Bas!

MACKIE: But when he saw our troops amass in force,
He shat himself in fear and ran like fuck
All cowardly in sobbing, shrieking voice –
Where once his kind had braved our Andy's face.

So, proudly then, once more, through Albion ran
The Brother-hooded Bravehearts. Full of fight.
From Albion tae Ingram, Candleriggs,
And down towards the Broomielaw we sped.
But nowhere could we find that fearty cunt.

The GANG roar in frustrated disappointment. One gang member jumps up on stage and mimes MACKIE's acount of Dunky's actions

MACKIE: Then Dunky said 'I cannae understaun
How such a muppet could gie' us the slip –
Cos he's a refuge newboy on the block
But we've lived here for years and know the place.' . . .

GANG: Aye!

MACKIE: Then Biscuit pipes up loud tae all the troops –
'See back on Stockwell Street? I saw a pair
Of lads that we should take, one black, one white,
Who looked at me, or gave me eye it seemed,
When I, wi' roasting speed, had passed them by.'

MACKIE: Then Stu, his voice all rage, gave out tae us,
And clearly could we hear his boiling wrath,
That now we must:
'those fucking cunts sort out.
Teach them tae eyeball us on Glasgow's streets.'

But. Even as he spoke tae spur us on,
Before we could turn round and hunt them down,
The very two we sought now crossed our path
By turning out from back the alley's way.

And straight away, in reflex tae their sight,

Kenzie launched a devastating fist,

GANG: Wooaahhhh!

MACKIE: That struck the darker coloured of the two,
And smashed the foreign structure of his face –
So blood poured out through shattered nose and mouth –
Enough tae drown the fucker where he stood,
Tho' he, instead just gasped and choked for breath.
Then, suffered Kenzie's boot into his baws
Wi' such a mortal cry of pain and grief
That several of our troop were stunned quite still,
But soon laughed loud, and cheered Great Kenzie's deed.

Laughs from GANG.

KENZIE: He's no so fucking sun-tanned handsome now
I've re-arranged the ugly fucker's face.

MACKIE: At which the troops, as one, took great delight
And made afresh their chants of mocking hate . . .

GANG: Go hame, ya cunts!
Go hame, ya cunts!

MACKIE: Now, in that moment whilst we were distract,
The white one – Jesus why did he do this? –
Pulled up his stricken pal and pressed his ear
Wi' calming words tae ease the gory pain,
He salvaged from our midst his hurtmost friend –
So ran the pair of them way up the street.
So racing after them we ran like wind,
Which fanned afresh our red-hot fires of rage
Tae all-consuming hatred in our minds.
A trail of flame and smoke we left behind
As comet-like, we rushed at fright'ning speed. Now –
Kenzie's awe-inspiring flaring eyes
Sought out, intae the streetlit darkness world.
And led us on, as leaders do, wi' words.

KENZIE: They're here! He's here! I smell his fucking stench
I'll tear the cunt apart when I lay hands.

MACKIE: Now. As he spoke, his hand pulled out The Blade
Which glinted through the dark in grievous spite:
And scored a thrill of terror in us all.
So round we ran, and round, and round again
All calling, screeching out in bloodlust thirst.
It wasnae us that ran – it was a force
Which in our hearts just had tae be obeyed.
Some thing, it was, in wild control a' us,
Which urged us on tae grave deeds of our fate.
Some God. Some Devil. Some fucking crazy power.
The spirit of Mad Dogs howled in our veins.
And, filled wi' it, I too ran fast along

While keeping closest touch tae Kenzie's side
Who all the time was raving on wi' this:

KENZIE: . . . He's here! he's here! No, fuck, he's gone! The cunt!
I'll fucking kill ya cunt, I'll slash your face . . .
I'll take your fuckin heid off where you stand, . . .
You Cuuuunnnnnnt!'

MACKIE: And now: the darkened world turned darker still.
As if the Gods would veil the dreadful night
In hope of blotting out what would occur.

For suddenly the white lad of the two,
Who blocked our path tae let his pal escape,
Now found himself wi' nowhere left tae hide –
Cos round him on all sides the troops stood firm.
So, in a desperate act tae break out free
He runs at me, as being tae his mind
The least, and weakest, of our warrior clan.
But, even as he raced tae where I stood
I felt a hand place lethal steel in mine
And in my ear was said –

KENZIE: Now here's your chance
Tae stick that cunt for good, he's coming now
He's coming at you now. *He's coming! now*!

MACKIE: **(to audience)** And all I did was lift my hand up . . . so.

MACKIE lifts his hands up suddenly, revealing the knife KENZIE has placed in it and freezes at the moment of fatal impact with the invisible victim. The GANG immediately run away, as fast as possible. The POLICE OFFICER walks on stage as MACKIE maintains his position, holding the knife with outstretched arm.

POLICE OFFICER: **(to audience)** What we have here is a knife that's penetrated the lad's chest between his ribs, and gone deep into the apex of his heart – an inch into the right ventricle, severing a coronary artery. In a matter of seconds his strong young heart will pump two pints of blood into his chest and lungs. He'll kind of drown. (**To MACKIE.**) You hear the gurgling. You feel every twitch and spasm as he slumps to the floor.

He's groaning and writhing, he's grabbed your blade. You feel his weight, don't you?

MACKIE: I don't feel nothing.

POLICE OFFICER: Don't you?

MACKIE: I didn't do nothing.

POLICE OFFICER: Didn't you? He's young, and strong, isn't he?

MACKIE: I don't know.

POLICE OFFICER: Make sure you look at him. *Look at him*!

MACKIE: He's too fucking heavy.

POLICE OFFICER: *Look at him*! He's looking straight at you.

MACKIE lifts his eyes to meet those of his victim.

POLICE OFFICER: You didn't know that when you stab someone, they look you right in the eye. Did you? What's he trying to say. He can't speak, his lungs are full of blood. He's asking you why is it that someone can take a knife and stick it in another person? Without any care for what will happen.

MACKIE: I didn't do it. I swear. It wasn't me.

POLICE OFFICER: Feel it? That dance of death on the end of your blade?

MACKIE: It's not my blade.

POLICE OFFICER: You've made it yours. *Do you feel it*?

MACKIE nods

POLICE OFFICER: All that trembling and jerking. Travels up the blade, doesn't it?

MACKIE: **(nods)** Uh-huh.

POLICE OFFICER: The convulsions of death, they are.

MACKIE: Ah Jesus, I can feel it.

POLICE OFFICER: You should be ashamed of yourself.

MACKIE: It's inside me!

POLICE OFFICER: I hope it's right inside you! I swear to God, you'll feel his heart jump and kick like a knackered washing machine.

MACKIE: No!

POLICE OFFICER: Doesn't matter what you've imagined beforehand or even how you've been trained, nothing can prepare you for the smell, or the sound, or the strange brotherly embrace of it once the blade's ripped Death into him.

MACKIE: He's eyeballing me.

POLICE OFFICER: He's eyeballing you alright. You're the last person he's ever going to see.

MACKIE: Shut up!

POLICE OFFICER: What's his poor mother going to say?

MACKIE: Shut up! Shut the fuck up!

POLICE OFFICER: What you going to do?

MACKIE: I don't know . . .

POLICE OFFICER: Are you going to leave it stuck in him or pull it out?

MACKIE: I don't know . . .

POLICE OFFICER: We'll find it if you leave it in him.

MACKIE: I'll pull it out.

POLICE OFFICER: He'll bleed buckets if you do.

MACKIE: I'll leave it in.

POLICE OFFICER: It's got your prints on it now.

MACKIE: I'll pull it out.

POLICE OFFICER: Make your fucking mind up. **(Beat.)** If you've got a fucking mind.

MACKIE drops the knife. It sticks in the floor with a sickening thud and stands on its point. MACKIE runs away, as fast as he can.

Scene 4

Flight from the Scene

MACKIE: I ran and ran and ran and retched dry puke.
I ran in sick'ning sweat and choking fear.
I ran, I fuckin ran as fast as dogs,
Wi' stabbing pains of stitches in my side.

But when I heard the distant sirens howl –
I gasped for breath and froze stock-still in fear.

Oh, get him tae that fuckin hospital!
And pull that knife from out his bleeding heart.
Don't let the fucker die. Don't let him die.

I never meant tae stab him. No. No way.
Kenzie put the knife . . . It wasn't me . . .
He just . . . He ran straight at me . . . I . . . I . . .

It's not the way you see it in the films –
A jab wi' blade, some blood, a wound that heals.

I felt the fucker's shattered heart explode;
He coughed his fuckin' lifeblood over me.

Don't let the fucker die. Don't let him die.
Don't let him die. Oh please. Don't let him die.

Scene 5

Forensics

POLICE OFFICER puts on a pair of forensic gloves.

POLICE OFFICER: His life was gone, of that there was no doubt,
No reflex in his pupils could we find,
No beat of life, nor any vital sound
Which might have murmured softly in his frame
To plead with us for paramedic aid.
So we left him laid out on the street
And wrestled with the despond of our minds.

Right. First we had to move the public back.
For tho' they were distressed and keen to help,
We have to keep you back – with plastic tape –
In case you should the evidence destroy.

So. Biologists arrived, from Scenes Of Crime,
Some fifteen minutes later, at the site.

They caref'ly laid out metal stepping stones,
Which keep the clues from damage underfoot.

Their touch on him was light, by glove and brush,
It was as if they thought he might awake
From slightest sensing of their careful hands.
But he lay still, insensible to all.

I couldn't help but stare at his young corpse –
What waste of life. For what? Just thrown away.
Thank God forensic tent was put in place
And swiftly hid his broken heart remains
From tearful eyes, and darkest thoughts of death,
And the prying fucking gaze of tabloid lens.

Great beams of light shone bright, around the tent,
From lanterns which we keep as part of plans
For nuclear war, or death of our young men.
They shine without the sunlight's warming grace,
And somehow make the night seem blacker yet
With ruthless beams of darkness visible.

Our work progressed with practised speed and skill
And detailed horror of this brutal act
Was brought from shadow into reason's light
Amid this callous glare of night made day.

Then, with conclusion reached, by expert team,
That all the evidence was now secured,
We moved him from the cold unyielding ground
To colder slab in city mortuary.

His phone and wallet spoke of who he was.
And gave his name to us indifferently
In Ozymandian facts of life now gone.
James.
Fairgrieve.
Student.

And so came time to do what we most dread.

For now the Crime Scene Manager had name,
A DOB, address and next of kin;
And, as we always do in suchlike case,
Two officers were quickly put in post,
Informed of that night's brutal act of death,
And swiftly sent to break the news to all
Unwitting family members at the home.

No matter what the time of day or night
Such news as this we tell immediately –
Even if its three a.m. we go.
Before the carrion press descend to feast
In howling packs at doors of grieving kin.
(He pulls the knife out of the floor.)
So, armed with new-honed details of events,
We went to pierce that heartfelt happiness
Which dwells within the breast of parent's love.

Scene 6

Where Now?

MACKIE: I ran and ran until my fuckin heart
Was bursting in my chest and in my ears.
I walked, I crawled, I tried tae pull in air –
Which made the bastard fires inside my lungs
Erupt, in flames of red hot agony.

He's dead. He must be stone cold fuckin dead.
I've killed that poor bastard – I don't know why.
I should have stayed – I might have saved his life.

I can't run any more, I just can't breathe.
My legs are pure dead fucking weights,
Afire wi' burning acid in my veins.

Ah Jesus Christ, the knife went in his heart!
I've got tae run and run and never stop!
I've got tae get away. I've got tae run.

But where? Oh, Fuckin Hell where can I go?
They'll come and get me if I go back home.

Oh Jesus cuntin Christ, just fuckin run!

Scene 7

The Knock on the Door

The MOTHER sits in a chair on stage.

POLICE OFFICER: I've lost count of how many times before
I've chapped on doors to bring this dreadmost news.
It must be more than nine or ten this year.
Experience, it seems, will never teach
An easy way to break a person's heart.

I'll go up to the house and say, quite calm,
'There's been a body found, and we believe
That it's your young son James, and that he's dead.'
And she'll say 'No, oh God, this cannot be.'

The MOTHER stands.

POLICE OFFICER: I'm DCI Martin Booth from Pitt St Police station. Are you Mrs. Alison Fairgrieve?

MOTHER: Yes. Is this about the Neighbourhood Watch?

POLICE OFFICER: I'm afraid not, this is in relation to another matter. Do you have a son James Fairgrieve?

MOTHER: He's not in trouble is he?

POLICE OFFICER: I'm sorry to say I've got some bad news for you. Would you please sit down.

To audience.

So now you wait and try your best to speak
With clear and simple words, of mortal woe.

To MOTHER who is now seated.

As I say we've got some news, and I'm afraid it's very bad news, and there's no easy way to say this, but, I believe that your son's been killed.

To audience.

No-one ever understands those words
Which say the thing that every parent dreads.
She'll answer straight away 'this cannot be . . .'

MOTHER: This must be a mistake. He's just gone into town with his friend . . .

POLICE OFFICER: Unfortunately we have strong cause to believe that is the case and that he is dead.

MOTHER: No, you've got it wrong. I spoke to James earlier this evening.

POLICE OFFICER: I'm afraid we know that. We checked his mobile and it shows he dialed your number here, just after six this evening. There was an incident at seven fifteen.

MOTHER: Incident? What incident? Where is he?

POLICE OFFICER: As I say, there was an incident and at the moment, Mrs. Fairgrieve, I'm sorry to have to tell you, James has been moved to the city mortuary.

MOTHER: No, that's not true. Take me to him. Please. I want to see him. I need to see him.

POLICE OFFICER: Of course.
(To audience.)
It is, in fact, required by law, that now
Post mortem should take place with speed,
To ascertain the cause of James' death.
And, this requires that people of his kin
Identify the body where it lies.
So now I have to take her to the morgue
To make her see, when I pull back the shroud,
That image of his face – bereft of life.
Then by her sob, or screams, or silent stare,
We'll know for sure exactly who he was.
(To MOTHER.)
I need to ask you to come and identify him.

MOTHER: Oh God . . .

POLICE OFFICER: I'm so sorry.

MOTHER: **(Suddenly shrieking and screaming.)**
No! No! What's happened? Oh God, not James! No! James! James! Oh please God, no.

Scene 8

The Book

MACKIE: I managed tae get home, back tae my house,
But thought the fuckin' police might be there
And so I hid, in fear and sweat, behind
The rubble of the knocked down factory.

Kenzie came and found me lying low
In trembling dread behind the concrete wall.
He hissed out, in the darkness, it was him –
I had no need tae fear his coming by.

To KENZIE

Is he dead?

KENZIE: He's fuckin dead as shit, I tell you mate,
He had a metal hard-on on his chest –
That knife stood up, erect and proud as fuck.

MACKIE: Ah Jesus, Jesus Christ, what can I do?

KENZIE: Get yer arse away from round this place.
The polis'll come for ye sure as fuck.
Some cunt'll grass, and blame it all on you
Cos they'll be feart in case they get the jail.

MACKIE: **(to audience)**
Once more he reached inside his trackie-top
But now, pulled out a book, and no a blade.
A Black book, small and hard, wi' 'lastic band,
All splattered brown and scarred wi' crusted blood.
(How quickly does blood turn from red tae brown?)

KENZIE: I picked this up, from where you stabbed that cunt.
It must have fallen out his pocket, mon.

MACKIE: O Jesus Christ, this book belonged tae HIM!
If only it had sat against his heart
And stopped the blade, he might be still alive.

KENZIE: It's full of writing! Aye! There's loads of shit;
Some fucking crap about the Greeks and Troy,
And other writing there – I read it all,
He's wrote in here the story of his life;
About his Maw and what she means tae him,
And stuff about him shagging this hot burd –
That's all wrote down here too. It's fucking cool.

MACKIE: And now, I felt some force inside me move.
It bled, like ice, deep down inside my guts –
A cold, clear rage that frosted up my heart
But left my mind as sharp as any knife.
That book was mine; I did the shameful deed
And, like the Spartans say in Gods Of Troy:
'The spoils of war belong tae those who slay'.

To KENZIE

Hey, Kenzie, gi' it here tae me, that's mine.

KENZIE: Away and shite, it's me that picked it up.

MACKIE: But only cos he lay dead on the ground.
I'm the one who stabbed him in the heart,
So anything of his – belongs tae me.

KENZIE: Go fuck yersel', I'm keeping this, awright?

MACKIE: **(to audience)**
And saying this, he stepped in shadow's way,
Which, like a hoodie pulled across his face
Concealed him from the lost look on my own.

But, as he went tae leave me there, so I
Was sudden filled wi' overwhelming Need –
Like junkies, who will do all desperate shite
Tae get their fix: That's how I was.

So when his back was turned, I ran at him,
And smacked him tae the floor wi' one hard skelp,

Then grabbed his head, and bounced it on the ground,
And found myself wi' knee pressed on his throat,
Which made him gasp and choke, wi' face all blue.

So mad was I wi' hunger and wi' fear,
I panned his face, full whack, wi' knuckled fist,
Again, again, again, I hit him hard,
Cos I knew, I was dead if he got up.
I pushed my knee, full force, tae burst the veins
That stood out on his fearsick face and neck,
Till blood and phlegm all gurgled down his throat.
Then, as I punched his face for one last time,
My thumb got jabbed, full deep intae his eye
Which burst, and sprayed it's gunge all over me.

KENZIE screams.

And he, in broken agony, lay still.

But I just took the book from out his grip,
And left him, barely breathing, on the ground.
Kenzie. Cunt. Who couldnae gi' a shit.
Well, I don't give a fuck about him now
I've got the book. This book. The life I took
All written down right here. Right in my hand.

Scene 9

Whose Tragedy?

POLICE OFFICER: **(to audience)**

You *never*, ever leave someone alone
To whom you've had to give such news as this.
You always ask for someone close to them
To sit in mournful shock, and attempt care.
But if that can't be done, you stay yourself
To keep them talking all the dark night long
In forlorn hope that it might do some good.
So it was I stayed through night's long hours
In listening to her griefstained words of woe,
Until the ill judged song of birds announced
Unwelcome greeting to the useless dawn.
Then came despairing friends and grieving kin,
Inept attendants on her sore distress.
Their clumsy silence brought her no relief.
I headed home.

He gets up, trying to contain his angry tears.

Listen.

These things that happen they're . . . horrific, they're tragic, but they're no my tragedy. That's the bottom line. You have empathy for people, compassion for them, but you don't take it home with you. My ex-wife told me that. Jesus, imagine if you took this home with you . . .

Scene 10

No Reasons

MACKIE is now despairingly drunk with a can of brew in hand.

MACKIE: I strayed into the land of NoReasons,
Tae scavenge on its empty plenty shelves
And stacks of sugared fats – pure fuckin filth –
That kills our pauperised, untutored kin
More surely than does knife or chib or blade;
Past dykes of wine and lager, ground tae sky,
All straining tae hold back their toxic flood;
Through sandbagged walls of crisps, and tartrazine
And EisenBrau and shit that we devour.
And easy fuckin pickings did I snatch,
So walked wi' brew in Jaket stashed away
Right up tae face security's old prick
Who, none the fuckin wiser, let me pass.

And looking back inside I saw a troop
Of old and glaikit bampots, stupit men
Who wander round the store wi' self-same walk,
The eunuch's shattered stumbling Baw-less gait.
They, waiting for bitch matriarchal word
Tae push their trolleys round from aisle tae aisle,
Do lumber in a sleeping scooby state,
Whilst she wi' full control directs his life.

'Ya fuckin Hyena ya, ya bitch, ya cow!'

Those neutered pricks wi' dead unseeing eyes,
In dead unliving bodies shackled so.
All ambling like the numpties in that film
Where, in a shopping Mall, some cunts get locked.

'Ye fuckin fearty pricks, ye shitebags ye'.

Are these real men? These Fathers? Leaders? Kings?
Who even on the telly are reviled
And mocked by adverts all – as bawless cunts.
What loss tae us if gelded sheep like these
In drunk or druggèd daze fall down and die?
If such moronic dreeks should come near me
They'll feel my blade burn through their bloated guts.

I've chibbed at nobler meat than theirs, and chewed
Through tougher of their fuckin' stupit kind
In burger bun;
'Ye useless fuckin cunts!'

Scene 11

Dog Borstal

POLICE OFFICER is in the pub, he has the remains of a pint of Guinness in his hand.

POLICE OFFICER: Dog Borstal, have you seen that on your screens? I love that bloody program. Tell you why.
It's mostly 'cos it says if you've a dog
But fail to treat it right, around it turns
And makes your life an abject misery
Of whining, barking, biting, howling rage.
That's not the poor dog's fault, the fault's your own;
That would not treat the beast with due respect,
Nor tender to its needs nor give due care,
But made a toy of him, as you saw fit.

So now you find he's pissing on your chips,
And bites yer arse when e'er he gets the chance.
Which tells you more than words of mine can say
About the need for care and for respect.

See . . .

There's this . . . grave . . . on Tumbledown. And in it is a . . . white, shrouded body. No coffin. But when you open the shroud – it's a beautiful Patagonian shroud – there's no corpse either, just two eyes. Pick up the eyes and you'll see the pupils are dilated wide with death. If you turn the eyes under the cold grey sunlight you can just make out a strange image inside. It's my ugly nineteen year-old face, screaming in rage as I twisted the bayonet – the last living thing that poor bastard ever saw. Imprinted on those retinas.

What are we like? Eh? Us fucking Scots? A swirl of the tartan; a skirl of the pipes; here's your blade; we're off to war – Hooray! The fucking Heart of Self-Lothian.

Scene 12

Petrol Station

MOTHER: I drove off, early next morning. Very early; I don't know two forty five? Three? After the identification I couldn't sleep at all.

I drove for miles and miles. Hours. Not knowing where I was going – in a kind of dream really. Trying to remember his face. He'd had so many faces – baby face, toddler face, twelve year old's, surly teenager face, young man's face with a bumfluff goatee . . . all him. But I couldn't work out which one was him. Which one I'd lost most.

God knows how I didn't hit anything because when I pulled in to the petrol station I realised I had no memory of how I got there. I had to ask the young man on the till where I was. I didn't quite hear what he said because I was thinking that he was probably five or six years older than James.

Turns out the garage was only four miles from where I live, but I'd been driving for nearly eight hours by then.

And then I asked the lad on the till where neds live.

He didn't understand, so I said. 'You know, neds? Where do they live? What areas do they live in?'

He said there were areas all over Glasgow, but thinking about it, wouldn't it be a great idea if ned areas were labelled in the AA map?

I said yes it would.

I didn't realise he was joking.

And then he suddenly asked, very gently, if he could phone someone for me. My husband? A family member?

His kindness upset me, so I said yes. Yes. Would you call James? Can you do that?

POLICE OFFICER: We got a call from a petrol station attendant at ten to eleven that morning. The young lad said, and these are his words, 'She's lost and she's lost it.'

Scene 13

The Burger Bar

The MOTHER enters with a cup of coffee in a paper cup.

All this is watched carefully by MACKIE.

MACKIE: Oh Fuck! I know exactly who she is:
His Ma. From that appeal on the TV.

She picks up the coffee and takes a sip, puts it back down on the table and looks around. In doing this she hits the table and the coffee spills. MACKIE who has been watching, jumps up and rescues the cup and quickly throws some serviettes across in the path of the coffee to stop it reaching her.

MOTHER: Thank you, so clumsy, I . . .

MACKIE: Cool, cool. I got it.

MOTHER: Thanks.

MACKIE: **(to audience)**
She's not like women that you see round here,
Who curse and wail, and screech aloud in angst
When, after sniffing cans, their kid's found dead.

To MOTHER

D'you want another one? I'll get one out of them for you.

MOTHER: No, it's ok, you've been very kind. Thank you.

MACKIE: **(to audience)**
She's full of grief and pain for her lost son –
Her sorrow makes her . . . beautiful, to me.

(To MOTHER) You famous?

MOTHER: No. I'm not famous.

MACKIE: I seen you on the telly but? On the news?
That student that got stabbed, you're his ma, int ya?

MOTHER nods.

MACKIE: You greeting?

MOTHER shakes her head.

POLICE OFFICER All her friends at home said not to come,
Or if she must, then not to go alone
To such a place as this where life is cheap.
Where 'Drunks and addicts wait on every street!'
Her friends all begged her stay, with pleading cries,
And all the time in tears, as if they felt
That she, by setting foot in Housing Scheme,
Was facing certain injury or death.
They even hid her car keys, just in case.

MOTHER: I had a spare.

POLICE OFFICER: She will not be denied.
She has the strength of purpose of The Damned
Who have to follow what is in their heart
No matter what the consequences be.

MACKIE: Why the fuck don't you just run out fast
And get the hell away from her right now?
It's bad enough tae live from day tae day
Wi' guilty fear and puking in your guts.
Why make it worse by gazing at her here?

I slashed those lines of grief into her face –
As deep and evermore as Andy's scars.

MACKIE goes to the table and sits beside her.

POLICE OFFICER: You're playing a dangerous game.

MACKIE: It's not a game.

POLICE OFFICER: Haven't you done enough to her?

MACKIE: I know what I done!

He puts down a handful of paper serviettes.

MACKIE: Here. They have them for the burgers.

She takes a serviette and wipes her nose. They sit at the table for a while without saying anything.

POLICE OFFICER: Go on then. Ask her. What's she doing here? Ask her.

MACKIE: You fucking ask her.

Silence.

MACKIE: Whit you doing here?

MOTHER: I came to see.

MACKIE: See whit?

MOTHER: I came to see what it's like in a place like this.

MACKIE: A place like this? You know this place?

MOTHER: No.

MACKIE: You reckon they come from here? D'wans who killed him?

MOTHER: Not here, no . . .

MACKIE: But a place like this?

MOTHER: I don't know.

MACKIE: Where do you live?

MOTHER: I don't want to . . .

MACKIE: It's not a place like this though, is it?

Beat.

MOTHER: No, I live . . . somewhere . . .

MACKIE: Better?

MOTHER: Else. I live somewhere else.

MACKIE: You've come here, tae a place like this and you're looking at people like us, because you're thinking it must be one of us that killed him. Cos we come from a place like this.

MOTHER: That's not what I meant.

MACKIE: It fucking is.

Beat.

MOTHER: Yes. Maybe it is.

Long Silence.

MACKIE: **(to audience)**
She's right, this is the very place indeed
Where you can find such murdering cunts as me.
This scummy, no-hope shit hole, left tae rot,
Where angry fuckers skulk around the place
Wi' desperation in their desperate minds,
In case a chance for something came their way.
What kind of chance do we have growing up,
All couldn't-give-a-fuck, in wasteland place?

POLICE OFFICER: You had a chance, but chose to take a knife
And thrust it deep into a young lad's heart.
Don't whinge and say the fault all lies elsewhere
'Cos at the crunch, you didn't give a shit.

MACKIE: Well, no-one gives a shit about this place
And no-one gives a shit for people here,
So I don't give a fuck for what you think,
Or any other cunt, Fuck you. Fuck you.

POLICE OFFICER: So why are you all wound up by the deed
If what you say is true in your defence?

MACKIE: Why don't you get the fuck tae Portugal?
Go find that girl who matters tae you all
And leave the dross like us tae drown in filth.
Your papers are nae full of how we must
In destitution live in gulag schemes,
You're only interested when little girls
From caring homes of comfort come to grief.
See we are bred in need and poverty
So she can live in comfort in her place.

POLICE OFFICER: Well, come on then, explain to her right now
The Class War justice of your murdering deed.
Go on.

MACKIE: **(to MOTHER)** You drive here?

MOTHER: Yes.

MACKIE: Is that your Jeep? The BM?

MOTHER: Yes.

MACKIE: Did you look out of the windae of that when you drove here?

MOTHER: I wasn't looking. I was upset I . . .

MACKIE: So you didnae see it get poorer and shittier and more fucked up as you drove here? You didnae see the nice big buildings and trees gradually turn intae fucking slums and shit holes?

MACKIE: **(to POLICE OFFICER)**
I bet she's got insurance on her car.
I bet she'll have insurance on her home.
I bet she's got a dog and that's insured;
She's taken steps tae guard against all harm:
Except – for when her son would meet wi' me.
Why the fuck did she not think of that!
A few quid spent insuring that this place
Could never breed young fucked-up men like me.
But cheaper tae get strong-arm pricks like you
Tae lock the stable door when damage done.

POLICE OFFICER: You're not alone in coming from this place,
There's loads of lads like you who live round here
Who never get in trouble with the law,
So don't go making claims to be Rob Roy
Or any kind of hero for your class.
I'm from such a run-down place as this
And there's no way that you speak up for me.

MACKIE: I bet you don't live round here anymore!

POLICE OFFICER: That's not the point! Keep sight of what you did; which simply put is slaughter, cold as day.
And though your life's been tough up to this point
Not everyone from here goes out and kills.

MOTHER: Why is it that someone can simply take a knife and stick it in another person? Without any care for what will happen. What's going on when something like that can come about? I'd better go.

MACKIE: No! No. Don't. Don't go.
Everything is fucked up. It's all fucked up and can't be put right.

POLICE OFFICER: **(taking the small black book out of MACKIE's top)** A reading from the Final Book of James.

MACKIE: You fuckin bastard!

POLICE OFFICER: **(opens it and reads)** 'There'll come a time . . .'

MACKIE: No, don't!

POLICE OFFICER: . . . when I will have to look
Upon my Mother's face when she is dead
It is the natural order of the world . . . '

He breaks off and puts the book back in MACKIE's top.

MACKIE: **(to MOTHER)** I'm sorry.

MOTHER: Why are you sorry?

MACKIE: Because you're right. About us. The kind of people that live here. It will be somebody from a place like this has killed him. Won't it? It always is. It'll be some cunt my age. Any of us. Look around. There, see? It could have been him that done it. Or him. Or him. You can't even be sure that's not the hand that killed him.

MACKIE holds his hand out to show her.

MOTHER: Oh God, Oh God. **(She takes his hand and kisses it.)**

I'm sorry, I'm really sorry. I'm sorry that things are the way they are. I'm sorry there's no justice in the way things are. And I'm sorry that I haven't given this a moment's thought til now.
But, please help me.
I need to know . . . what it was like, for him, to die, to die like that, on the street, alone.

Without friends or fam . . .
I just can't stop thinking . . .
I can't bear the . . .
It . . .
I need to know if he said anything. At the end.
He must have known he was going to die.
I know he wouldn't have been able to say much, because of all the blood in his lungs, the police told me that. They said he wouldn't have been able to speak.
But he might. He might have said something . . .
He might have. I need to know. I have to know.

MACKIE: You'd have tae ask the bloke that stabbed him.

MOTHER: Or maybe someone who was just there. maybe not even in the gang, not meaning to do any harm.
I'm not here to get anyone.
My James is dead. That won't change.
But if I could find out what he said I'd give anything for that.
Just another moment of contact. Before he fades into the past.
I don't need someone to go to jail for it. Some young lad who never had a chance . . .
I just need to know . . .

Beat.

MACKIE: He was trying to save his pal wasn't he? When he got stabbed.

MOTHER: Yes. He was.

MACKIE: They said that on the news.
I couldn't have done what he did – stand up for a pal against someone wi' a knife. That takes real balls. He was – brave.

MOTHER: Yes, he was brave.
Thank you.
Are you brave?

MACKIE: What d'ya mean?

MOTHER: How would your mum feel if you died like that?

MACKIE: My Maw? What would you know about my Maw? She's not a mum like you. Your face is all posh but my maw's is all boney. And even when she's no sucking on a ciggy her face's still all pulled in. You smell like soap, but she smells of fags. And you're clean, but my Maw will never get clean. When she was smashed she telt us tae get tae fuck, and when she was sober she telt us tae get tae fuck. It was only when she was greeting about some shit or other she'd say she loved us all. Ma sister had tae feed me and wash me and look out for me.

MOTHER: But if your mum asked you for something to make her life bearable, you'd give it to her, wouldn't you?
Or your sister – if she was a mother to you.

MACKIE: What's so special about mothers, anyway? They say they love their kids. That's just shite. The fuckin telly's full of it and it's fuckin shite. Mothers are just people and they're as fucked up as everybody else, and they fuck their kids up or they treat them like fashion accessories or pets.
But kids do love their maws. No matter how fucked up or mean or selfish or posh they are. It's the kids who always love their maws.
Does that help you?

Silence.

I'm gonnae go.

MOTHER: No! Please. Don't go. Don't leave me.
Please . . .

They look hard at each other.

After a little while MACKIE reaches into his top and takes out

JAMES' bloodstained black notebook and puts it on the table in front of her.

She recognises it at once.

Scene 14

Funeral Pyre

POLICE OFFICER appears in light on one part of the stage. He looks directly at the MACKIE similarly lit in another. They look hard at each other throughout.

POLICE OFFICER: Days later, in the Glasgow mournful air,
The people gathered round the funeral pyre
Of our sad city's latest fallen son.
They quenched the fun'ral flames with tears of grief,
Then took away his ashes in an urn
And placed them in a grave upon the hill,
Which gates they locked,
In hope to keep at bay
Such 'scum' as them, who might deface the stones.
And so they left and gathered in her house,
To mourn, in sad remembrance of a son.
Then closed her door and headed, all, away;

Blackout.

The End